News
Nonfiction Readers

W9-BQS-896

The Moon

by
Melanie Chrismer

Children's Press
An Imprint of Scholastic Inc.
New York Toronto London Auckland Sydney
Mexico City New Delhi Hong Kong
Danbury, Connecticut

These content vocabulary word builders
are for grades 1–2.

Consultant: Michelle Yehling, Astronomy Education Consultant

Photo Credits:

Photographs © 2008:Corbis Images: 2, 5 top left, 15 (Buzz Aldrin/Original image courtesy of NASA), 19 (Richard T. Nowitz); Holiday Film Corp.: back cover; NASA: 1, 4 top, 5 bottom right, 5 bottom left, 7, 11, 13, 17, 23; Photo Researchers, NY: cover (John Bova), 20, 21 (Fred Espenak), 4 bottom left (John Foster), 4 bottom right, 5 top right, 9 (Detlev van Ravenswaay).

Book Design: Simonsays Design!
Book Production: The Design Lab

Library of Congress Cataloging-in-Publication Data
Chrismer, Melanie.
The moon / by Melanie Chrismer.—Updated ed.
  p. cm.—(Scholastic news nonfiction readers)
  Includes bibliographical references and index.
  ISBN-13: 978-0-531-14699-6 (lib. bdg.)   978-0-531-14764-1 (pbk.)
  ISBN-10: 0-531-14699-5 (lib. bdg.)   0-531-14764-9 (pbk.)
  1. Moon—Juvenile literature. I. Title.
  QB582.C54 2008
  523.3—dc22   2006102791

CONTENTS

WORD HUNT

Look for these words as you read. They will be in **bold**.

astronauts
(**ass**-truh-nawts)

satellite
(**sat**-uh-lite)

solar system
(**soh**-lur **siss**-tuhm

4

footprint
(**foot**-print)

orbit
(**or**-bit)

spacecraft
(**spayss**-kraft)

space suit
(spayss soot)

5

The Moon!

Can you jump on
the Moon?

Yes, if you can get there.

The Moon is far away. It
would take three days to
get there from Earth.

The Moon is about 238,855 miles (384,400 kilometers) away from Earth.

The Moon is an object that circles around Earth. The path it takes is called its **orbit**.

The Moon is not a planet. It is a **satellite**.

Earth and the other planets in the **solar system** go around the Sun.

Sun

Earth

Moon

The Moon takes 28 days to travel around Earth.

Everyone can see the Moon from Earth.

But only twelve people have walked or jumped on the Moon.

That's not a lot!

You can only go to the Moon by flying in a **spacecraft**.

In 1969, NASA sent three **astronauts** to the Moon.

They went in a spacecraft called *Apollo 11*. Mike Collins flew the craft.

Neil Armstrong and Buzz Aldrin got to walk on the Moon.

Neil Armstrong, Mike Collins, and Buzz Aldrin

Neil Armstrong was the first human to step on the Moon.

He made the first **footprint**!

His footprint will be there for more than a million years.

There is no wind on the Moon to blow it away.

This is Neil Armstrong's footprint on the Moon.

The Moon has no air.

An astronaut must wear a **space suit**.

The Moon is very cold in the shade and very hot in the sunlight.

A space suit keeps you just right to jump on the moon!

backpack

The backpack has air in it so the astronaut can breathe.

You don't need a space suit to jump on Earth.

You can have fun jumping on the Moon if you go to a space camp!

Look at him jump!
He is at a space camp.

MOON PHASES

When the Moon travels around Earth, the part we see changes shape. We call each change a phase.

WANING ⟵

Next month, look at the Moon every night. If you are seeing less of it as each night passes, the moon is waning.

WAXING

If you are seeing more of it as each night passes, the moon is waxing.

YOUR NEW WORDS

astronauts (**ass**-truh-nawts) people
trained to travel in space

footprint (**foot**-print) a mark made by
a shoe or the foot of a person or an
animal

orbit (**or**-bit) the path an object takes
around another object

satellite (**sat**-uh-lite) an object that circles
a larger object

solar system (**soh**-lur **siss**-tuhm) the
group of planets, moons, and other
things that travel around the Sun

space suit (spayss soot) special clothing
to wear in space

spacecraft (**spayss**-kraft)
a vehicle that astronauts use to fly
into space and study space